With the certainty of a storyteller & the faith of a poet, Florian Vetsch's *The Flaying of Marsyas* reassures that memory is a lens on the future, a navigation between relinquishing & claiming, a letter stamped but not yet addressed. Love sustains, sound transports, relics divinize, on a binge of lively poems that celebrate the unsettling & the unforseen. we are warned in Douglas Spangles' coaxing translations. The death of a martyr, a long bake in the sauna, an eye of light cast the future ablaze. "Drive slowly / Deer wander here!"

— *Caroline Reul, poet, translator, In the Morning We Are Glass/ Am Morgen sind wir aus Glas*

Florian Vetsch Portrait, *Tamea Wissmann*

Ein Cross-over-Ritt aus Hochkultur und Beat-Gedichten voller Erinnerungen und Visionen, Zärtlichkeiten und Witz, geschrieben mit den fetzenden Schnitten von Heute. Die Sammlung „*Die Häutung des Marsyas*" taucht in Geschichte und Geschichten ein und feiert die nackte Gegenwart.

A cross-over ride of high culture & beat poems full of memories & visions, tenderness & wit, written with today's raging cuts. *The Flaying of Marsyas* collection delves into history & stories, & celebrates the bare present.

> — *Clemens Umbricht, Swiss poet & translator, author, „Das Alphabet des Archæopteryx"*

He carries the flameless flame: "Poesy especially speaks prophecies..."

> — *Louise Landes Levi,* poet, author, *The Water Mirror*

Reading *The Flaying of Marsyas* is like taking a pilgrimage through poetry into stirring new territory. These poems satisfy my hunger for splendor and simplicity and my thirst for the mystical & the miraculous. In the end, they offer a consoling verdict on reality. From the "stillness in falls of snowdrift" to the "wisdom & power & art," this is a splendid book.

> — *David Biespiel,* poet, essayist, critic, author, *Republic Café, Wild Civility,* former editor, *Poetry Northwest*

Reprobate/GobQ Books
Portland OREGON 97211

2024

The flaying of Marsyas:

Selected Poems

Florian Vetsch

Eng Tr., Douglas Spangle

DiE HäUTUNg DES MaRSyaS: AUSGEWÄHLTE GEDICHTE, FLORIAN VETSCH ////|||\\\ ThE FlAyING Of MaRSyaS: SELECTED POEMS, FLORIAN VETSCH; ENG TR., DOUGLAS SPANGLE ////|||\\\ SELECTED CROATIAN TR., Ana Katana, Jelena Pataki SELECTED SPANISH TR., rvb, T. Warburton y Bajo & Lyda Alvarez

THIS IS A REPROBATE BOOK PUBLISHED BY GOBQ BOOKS

ISBN 979-8-88526-355-9 \\// $ 18.oo

International distribution: Ingram Spark /\\ Digital Edition Pending

10 9 8 7 6 5 4 3 2 1

Die Häutung Des Marsyas / The Flaying of Marsyas
Copyright © 2024, Florian Vetsch; English translation,
Copyright © 2024, Douglas Spangle

Selectec Croatian translations: O staroj fotografiji, Copyright © 2024, Ana Katana; Jackie Brown, Stara ljubavna Copyright © 2024, Jelena Pataki

Selected Spanish translations: Con respecto a una vieja fotografía, Jackie Brown, Un tarde con Ed Sanders,* Copyright © 2024, rvb & T. Warburton y Bajo; Vieja canción de amor, Copyright © 2024, rvb, T. Warburton y Bajo & Lyda Alvarez

1st. printing, published Jan. 2024, Reprobate/GobQ Books, GobQ L.L.C., 338 NE Roth, Portland OR 97211

Several pomes fr. this collection have appeared in Gobshite Quarterly, (incl. the English, Spanish & Croatian translations); full publication history & credits incl. on pgs. no. 60—61

DIE HÄUTUNG DES MARSYAS:
Ausgewählte Gedichte: Florian Vetsch

○ ○ ○ ○ ○ ○ ○ ○ ○ ○ ○ ○ ○ ○ ○ ○ ○ ○ ○ ○

Inhalt

○ ○ ○ ○ ○ ○ ○ ○ ○ ○ ○ ○ ○ ○ ○ ○ ○ ○ ○ ○

THE FLAYING OF MARSYAS:
Selected Poems: Florian Vetsch

(tr. fr. the German, Douglas Spangle)

○ ○ ○ ○ ○ ○ ○ ○ ○ ○ ○ ○ ○ ○ ○ ○ ○ ○ ○

Contents

Índice de contenidos

○ ○ ○ ○ ○ ○ ○ ○ ○ ○ ○ ○ ○ ○ ○ ○ ○ ○

*) *Traducción, T. Warburton y Bajo y rvb;*
**) *Traducción, T. Warburton y Bajo y rvb*
   y Lyda Alvarez

Sadržaj

○ ○ ○ ○ ○ ○ ○ ○ ○ ○ ○ ○ ○ ○ ○ ○ ○ ○

‡) *Prijevod, Ana Katana;*
‡‡) *Prijevod, Jelena Pataki*

Ein Gedicht

Das Aufschneiden
französischer Broschuren
zur Hälfte nur.
Ein Brief ohne Adresse, frankiert.

Das Rauschen
in deinen Röcken, ein Knistern
ein Flaum.

Schlingernder Buchenzweig auf dunklen Wassern.

Kinderschritte auf dem Kies
eine Rassel, Scheite
schwirrende Sommervögel.

Die Stille im Fallen der Schneeflocken.

Eine Münze im Hosensack
eine Haschischkrume
ein Speisekraut.

A Poem

Just cutting
French brochures
in half.
A letter without an address, stamped.

The rustle
in your skirts, a crinkle
a fluff.

Swinging beech twig on dark waters.

Children's tread on the gravel
a rattle, wood chips
whirring birds of summer.

The stillness in falls of snowdrift.

A coin in the pants pocket
a crumb of hashish
a dish of greens.

Auf eine alte Fotografie

Meine Mutter hält
auf der gezahnten schwarz-weiss Fotografie
den Hörer an die Ohrmuschel, blickt
nach links in die Höh
die Haartolle, die kurzärmlige weisse Rüschenbluse
Schürze & Rock verschieden gepunktet
schmale Damenarmbanduhr
der Holztisch vor ihr leer
so geschäftig sieht sie aus, so tüchtig
das Leben liegt vor ihr, kaum 20 Jahre alt
draussen tobt Hitler
die Kartoffeln holt meine Mutter in der
       Anbauschlacht
mit denselben Händen ein
mit denen sie jetzt den Hörer hält, zart
mit der Linken
den einzigen Liebsten im Herzen

Im Bildrand rechts verschwindet die Strippe

On an Old Photograph

My mother holds
in the serrated black & white photograph
the receiver to her ear, glances
to the left in the height
of her hairdo, the short-sleeved ruffled white
blouse apron & skirt polka-dotted
slim lady's wristwatch
the wooden table before her bare
she seems so busy, so capable
that life lies ahead of her, just 20 years old
Hitler rages abroad
my mother holds the potatoes in the harvest
     campaign
with the same hands
which she now holds the receiver, soft
in her left
the only favorite in her heart

In the margin right the cord vanishes

Con respecto a una vieja
fotografía

Mi madre tiene
en la fotografía serrada a blanco y negro
el auricular a su oído, mirando
a la izquierda a la altura
de su peinado, la blusa blanca de olanes
y manga corta delante al y falda de lunares
reloj de pulsera delgado para dama
la mesa de madera desnuda frente a ella
y se vé tan ocupada, tan capaz, toda su vida
por delante, apenas veinte años de edad
Hitler ruge en el extranjero
mi madre agarra las patatas de la cosecha en
          campaña
con las mismas manos con las
que ahora toma el auricular, suave
a su izquierda
lo único favorito en su corazón

En el margen derecho el cordón se desvanece

**O staroj
fotografiji**

Moja majka drži
Na toj staroj, nazubljenoj, crnobijeloj fotografiji
slušalicu uz uho, te gleda
lijevo u visini
svoje frizure, bijela bluza na volane kratkih
        rukava
pregača & suknja na točkice
tanašan damski sat na ruci
drveni stol prazan pred njom
djeluje tako zauzeto, tako sposobno
život je čeka, tek joj je 20
Hitler hara po inozemstvu
moja majka drži žetvene krumpire
tim istim rukama
kojima sada drži slušalicu, nježno
u lijevoj
jedinog koji joj je srcu mio

Na rubu desne margine iščezava žica

Jackie Brown

Pam! & dem Drecksack die Birne
Mit der Pumpgun weggeblasen
Oder auch Ordell mit der Knarre &
Mit Worten paralysiert — nach dem Krebs.

Ach Jackie, Foxy dear, Friday my
Räum doch mal im Parlament, beim
    Steueramt
& den Medienkonzernen auf! Auch dabei
    hättest du
Nicht nur die Farbigen hinter dir.

Jackie Brown

Pam! & the scumbag's gourd
Blown away with the pumpgun
Or Ordell too with the rod &
Paralyzed with words — after the cancer.

Oh Jackie, Foxy dear, Friday my
Search in Parliament surely, at the Tax
    Office
& the media concerns! And there you'd
    have
Not just the colored people behind you.

Roy Lichtenstein

Jackie Brown

Pam! y el cráneo del cerdo
volado con la escopeta
o también Ordell con la fusta y
paralizado con palabras, después del cáncer.

Ah Jackie, sexy querida, el viernes mi
busqueda en el Parlamento sin duda, en la oficina de
    impuestos
y los medios de comunicación! Y tendrías
no sólo la gente de color dándote apoyo.

Jackie Brown

Pam! i glavu nitkova
Raznijela je sačmarica
Ili i Ordell s bičem i
Paralizirao riječima — poslije raka.

O, Jackie, seksi maco, u petak moja
Čistka u Parlamentu stoji, u poreznom uredu
I korporativnim medijima! I tamo uz tebe
Ne bi bili samo ljudi druge boje.

Altes Liebeslied

Variation über A Case of You *von*
Joni Mitchell

Du lehrst meine Feder reisen
Du lässt meine Quelle springen
Du machst meine Schlange steigen
Du singst wie Wein in meinem Kopf
Schwer, bitter & süss

& tränke ich ein ganzes Fass von dir
So stände ich noch immer aufrecht hier

Du teilst deine Decke mit mir
Du steckst den Finger in mein Seel
Du perlst aus diesen Zeilen quer
& singst wie Wein in meinem Kopf
Schwer, bitter & süss

& tränke ich ein ganzes Fass von dir
So stände ich noch immer aufrecht hier

& tränke ich ein ganzes Fass von dir
So stände ich noch immer aufrecht hier

Old Love Song

Variation on *A Case of You* by
Joni Mitchell

You teach my pen to travel
You let my wellspring water
You make my serpent rise
You sing like wine in my head
Heavy, bitter & sweet

& if I drank a whole cask of you
So I'd still be standing here upright too

You share your blanket with me
You put a finger in my soul you do
Sparkling slant out of these lines
& sing like wine in my head
Heavy, bitter & sweet

& if I drank a whole cask of you
So I'd still be standing here upright too

& if I drank a whole cask of you
So I'd still be standing here upright too

Vieja canción de amor:

Variación de *A Case of You*
de Joni Mitchell

enseñas a mi pluma a viajar
dejas a mi manantial agua dar
contigo mi serpiente se endereza
cantas como vino en mi cabeza
pesado, amargo y dulce

y si bebí un barril entero de tí
y todavía estoy parado también aquí

conmigo tu cobija compartes
un dedo en mi alma pones
haces brillantes inclinaciones
de estas líneas
y mi cabeza como vino cantas canciones
pesado, amargo y dulce

y si bebí un barril entero de tí
y todavía estoy parado también aquí

y si bebí un barril entero de tí
y todavía estoy parado también aquí

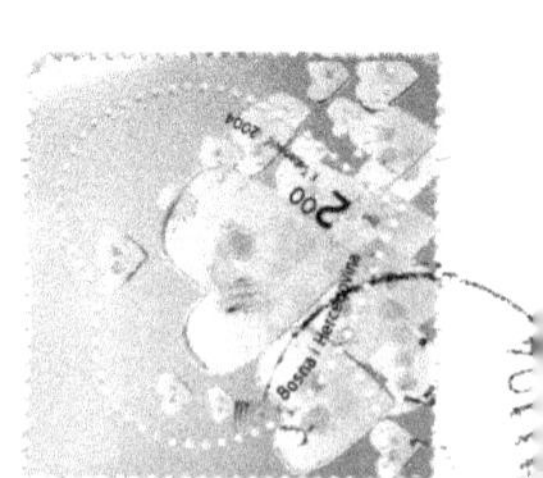

Stara ljubavna pjesma

Varijacija na *A Case of You*
od Joni Mitchell

Učiš moje pero da plovi
I moj izvor da poteče
Tjeraš moju zmiju da se digne
Pjevaš poput vina u mojoj glavi
Opojno, gorko i slatko

& sve da popijem cijelo bure tebe
Čvrsto bih na nogama ostao
Dijeliš svoju deku sa mnom
I da, zabijaš mi prst u dušu
Pokatkad mi koso bljesneš iz stiha
& pjevaš poput vina u mojoj glavi
Opojno, gorko i slatko

& sve da popijem cijelo bure tebe
Čvrsto bih na nogama ostao

& sve da popijem cijelo bure tebe
Čvrsto bih na nogama ostao

Ein Nachmittag bei Ed Sanders

Woodstock, 19. April 2010

Fahren Sie langsam
Hier wandeln Hirsche!
Für sie errichtet er Zäune
Um die Blumenbeete, streut
Maiskörner. Do you
Know Sharon Tate?
Ich brauche Polanski nicht
Dafür – auch den Papst nicht
Die Polizeiberichte genügen
& die Erinnerung derer
Die mit mir alt geworden sind
12 Vogelarten zählt die Stubenuhr
Der Wellensittich & der Kakadu
Intervenieren, auch Islands
Vulkanasche. Globen, Schatullen
Regale – Bücher von Ginzy
Bis Stravinsky. Ein Harmonium
Ein Aquarium, überall
Pflanzen. "Seit 1958 sind wir
Zusammen & er ist noch
Immer ein Mysterium", lacht
Miriam. Be Free! SyQuest
Das Problem der Archivierung –
Fahren Sie langsam
Hier wandeln Hirsche!
Schwarze Turnschuhe, schwarze Jeans
Schwarzes Jacket, weisser Sticker:
Imagine Peace
Ihn sticht der Gift-Efeu nicht.

An Afternoon with Ed Sanders

Woodstock, 19. April 2010

Drive slowly
Deer wander here!
He sets up fences for them
Around the flower beds, scatters
Kernels of corn. Do you
Know Sharon Tate?
I need no Polanski
For that — nor the Pope
The police reports suffice
& the memory of those
Who have grown old with me
The parlor clock counts 12 species of birds
The parakeet & the cockatoo
Intervene, also Iceland's
Volcanic ashes. Globes, caskets
Bookcases — books from Ginzy
to Stravinsky. A harmonium
An aquarium, plants
everywhere. "Since 1958 we've been
Together & he's still
Always a mystery," laughs
Miriam. Be Free! SyQuest
the problem of archiving —
Drive slowly
Deer wander here!
Black tennis shoes, black jeans
Black jacket, white sticker:
Imagine Peace
The poison ivy does not sting him.

Una tarde con Ed Sanders

Woodstock, 19. Abril de 2010

Maneje despacio
¡Los ciervos vagan por aquí!
Él les pone bardas
alrededor de las flores, esparce
granos de maíz. ¿Conoce usted
a Sharon Tate?
No necesito a Polanski
para eso — ni al Papa
Los reportes de policía son suficientes
y la memoria de aquellos
quienes han envejecido conmigo
El reloj de la sala cuenta doce especies de aves
El perico y la cacatúa
intervienen, también las cenizas volcánicas
de Islandia. Globos, ataúdes
Estanterías — libros de Ginzy
a Stravinsky. Un armonio
Un acuario, plantas
por todas partes. *"Desde 1958 hemos
estado juntos y él es todavía siempre
un misterio,"* se ríe
Miriam. ¡Ser libre! *"SyQuest"*
el problema del archivado —
Maneje despacio
¡Los ciervos vagan por aquí!
Zapatos de tenis negros, jeans negros
Chaqueta negra, con calcamonia blanca:
Imagina la paz
la hiedra venenosa no le pica.

CUBA
Correos 2002
Autos Antiguos
HAB
15
Cadillac 1959, modelo Fleetwood

Die toten Dichter

Die toten Dichter pochen an meine Tür
Klingeln, begehren Einlass –
Für sie stehen meine Angeln immer offen

Sie räumen meinen Kühlschrank leer
Fischen sich meine Bücher aus den Regalen
Fläzen sich auf mein Sofa

Sie schalten meinen Computer ein
Blättern in meinen Dateien
Hören sich meine CDs an

Die toten Dichter schlafen in meinem Bett
Ziehen mir das Laken weg
Dringen in meine Träume ein

Käme ich denn ohne die toten Dichter je zur
        Ruhe?

The Dead Poets

The dead poets knock on my door
Ring, demand entrance —
For them my hinges often stand open

They clear out my refrigerator
Fish my books from the shelves
Flop on my sofa

They activate my computer
Go through the pages of my files
Listen to my CDs

The dead poets sleep in my bed
Pull the bedsheets from me
Intrude into my dreams

Would I come to rest without the dead
      poets?

Der Stein

Prag, 29. Mai 2013

Als Tautropfen in einer Rose
Hatte sich der Tod von Rabbi Löw versteckt
Dargeboten von seiner jüngsten Enkelin

Die Buchstaben auf der Stirn des Golems
Hatte er längst gelöscht & seine anderen Golems
Die Bocherim, in die Welt geschickt

Sie hatten auf ihn getrunken & auch ich tat
Heute einen Stein auf sein Grab
Gleich unter dem zum Pinienzapfen

Aufsteigenden Löwen, einen langen flachen
Stein, dunkel mit weisser Äderung
& von feiner, zarter Oberfläche

Ich hatte ihn lange im Hosensack getragen
Zur Erinnerung an einen Nachmittag, auch
Seiner schönen Form wegen & um beim Nachdenken

Mit ihm zu spielen... Nun träumt der Stein den Rabbi.

The Stone

Prague, May 29th 2013

As a dewdrop in a rose
Death hid itself away from Rabbi Löw
Presented by his youngest grand-daughter

At last he had effaced
The letters on the brow of the Golem & sent
His other Golems, the Bocherim, into the world

They drank to him & so today
I set a stone on his grave
Just underneath the pine cone

Rearing lion, a long flat
Stone, dark with white veins
& a fine, soft surface

I'd carried it in my pants pocket a long time
In memory of an afternoon, also
because of its fine form & to reflect on it

While turning it over . . . Now the stone dreams of
    the Rabbi.

Intermezzo

X-Ray & Man Ray trafen einander
Im Café Flore, Paris 1949
Sie setzten einander
Le Deuxième Sexe auseinander
& tranken Pastis: Kiki
Komplett durchleuchtet!

Intermezzo

X-Ray & Man Ray got together
At Café de Flore, Paris 1949
They sat together, made an
Exegesis of Le Deuxième Sexe
& drank Pastis: Kiki
Totally lit up!

**Blaubeerenparadies
ungestillt**

Der Kühlschrank ist immer
Eine gute Entschuldigung

Myrtillen mit Crème fraiche
Gar mehr als das –

Zuerst an den Kühlschrank
Dann unter die Decke

& aus dem Traumgeflecht
Wieder zum Kühlschrank…

Derart ergänzen sich
Feuer & Eis

**Blueberry Paradise
Unfulfilled**

The refrigerator is always
A good excuse

Myrtilles à la crème fraîche
Even more than that—

First to the fridge
Then under the covers

& then from the web of dreams
Back to the fridge . . .

Thus complete
Fire & ice

Bier-Gedicht

für Christoph Keller

Pfff-tok!
Kracht's bei der nächsten
Wie bei der Dose vorhin

Das Boot wässern
Kurz aufs Sprungbrett stehen
Schluck um Schluck
Die Flugroute nach oben korrigieren

Sich für einen Moment entschuldigen
Um den Himmel zu küssen
Excuse me while I kiss the sky

Thors Hammer schwingen
Mit einem Nuckeln am Horn
Die Ebbe einläuten
Unten auf der Erde

Den Brand am Morgen löschen, dann
Nebst Alka-Seltzer, die beste Medizin:
Pfff-tok!

Beer Poem

for Christoph Keller

Pfff-tok!
Make it to the next one
Like the can before

Soak the boat
Standing briefly on the divingboard
Gulp by gulp
Correcting the flight path upwards

Excuse yourself for a moment
To kiss the sky
Excuse me while I kiss the sky

Swinging Thor's hammer
With a pull at the horn
To sound the ebb
Down on earth

To put out the fire in the morning, then
Next to Alka-Seltzer, the best medicine:
Pfff-tok!

17 Minuten in der Sauna

& schnell fällt die Tür ins Schloss

Oglala Inikare, Weidenzweige als Weltgeviert, steiniger
   Mittenherd

Sanduhrzeit

Also die Skythen brannten unter Filzdecken den
   ganzen Hanf auf einmal ab & heulten
     dabei laut; nichts Hellenisches sei ihrer
      Schwitzjurte gleichgekommen, befand Herodot

Vorgänsehaut, die Haare stellen sich auf

& in Alexandria zerstoben während 6 langen
   Monaten die Schriftrollen der Grossen
     Bibliothek in den Bädern zu Dampf, mutierten zu
     Schweiss

Rinnsale durch Pigmentschrunden, Pergamentlachen

Oder jener einfache Hammam in Marrakesch, wo der
   Masseur dir auf den erhitzten
     Fliesen die Knie durchbiegt &
      Ohrmuscheln & Zehenzwischenräume auswäscht

Wasser in der Schulterkuhle

17 Minutes in the Sauna

& the door falls fast into the lock

Oglala Inikare, willow twigs as the quartered
    world, stony central hearth

Sand-clock time

So the Scythians burned the hemp entire
    beneath the felt blanket and shouted aloud;
    nothing of the Hellenes compared with
    their sweat yurt, Herodotus thought

Gooseflesh, the hair standing straight up

& in Alexandria for 6 long months the scrolls
    from the great library dispersed to vapor in
    the baths, changed to sweat

Runnels through flakes of pigment, parchment
    puddles

Or that simple hammam in Marrakesh, where
    on the heated tiles the masseur bends your
    knees & washes out the pavilion of ears &
    the space between the toes

Water in the shoulder hollows

In Finnland Met & Schnee, das Eismeer, ansonsten
    ist es dort heiss nur unter den Röcken

Seliges Triefen, salzige Kläranlage,
    Sammeltropfbecken

Bambusflötenmusik in Amsterdam,
    Lautstärkeskala 0,5 — die Holländer ächzen &
    hecheln, was die Lunge hält, das Nervengeäst,
    das Wundernetz

Aufheizen bis aufs Mark / Kratzen, schaben in der
    Entschlackungsmaschine

Soll der ganze Dreck man ab, dies alles wirst du eh
    verlassen müssen, es lassen, lassen

Die Schädeldecke zittert unterm Kopfhaar, platzt
    fast –

Das Balkenstarke stirbt keinen guten Tod,
    Weidenzweige vielleicht

& schnell fällt die Tür ins Schloss.

In Finland mead and snow, the icy sea, or else it is
    just hot there under the skirts

Blessed trickle, salty collection pond, watersaving
    bowl

Bamboo flute music in Amsterdam, volume set to 0.5
    — the Dutch wheeze and hack up what the lungs
    hold, the branches of nerves, retes mirabiles

Heating up till it's on the mark / Scratching, scraping
    in the detox machine

All the grunge absolves you, all this you must leave
    behind, leave it, leave it

The blanket of cranium quivers under your hair,
    almost explodes —

The roofbeams don't die a good death, willow twigs
    maybe

& the door falls fast into the lock

Die Häutung des Marsyas

Die Häutung des Marsyas gestaltete
Sich schwieriger als angenommen
Die lederne Haut des Satyrs liess
Sich nur schwer vom Fleisch schaben
Die Schindung dauerte Stunden –
Im Blutstrom sollen die Marterer
Nach der Vollendung ihres Werks
Gebadet haben; Apollo hatte sich längst
Abgewandt. Eisenoxid
Sickert aus dem Quellgebiet des Mäanders
Durch die Äonen. Al Hallaj feierte
Die höhere Begattung, den Flammentod
Des Falters, als ihm Arme und Beine
Vom Rumpf gehackt wurden
Mit einem Stumpf krakelte er
Sein letztes Selbstbildnis
In den Sand, leuchtend rot – auch
Sein Blut wusch die Täter nicht
Rein. Vor der Verbrennung
In Rom fixierten die Folterknechte
Giordano Brunos Zunge, die Räte wollten
Nicht, dass er noch zum Volk sprach
Raubten sein letztes Wort. Das beweist
Er hatte Recht: Sie hatten Grund
Sich mehr zu fürchten als er.

The Flaying of Marsyas

The flaying of Marsyas proceeded
With more difficulty than anticipated
The leathered skin of the Satyr only allowed
Itself to be peeled from the meat with effort
The stripping took hours —
The torturers were to have bathed
In the stream of blood after the completion
Of their labors; Apollo finally
Turned away. Iron oxide trickled
From the site of the Meander's source
Through the aeons. Al Hallaj celebrated
The higher wedding, the death in flames
Of the moth, while arms and legs
Were hacked from his trunk
He scrawled with a dull blade
His last self-portrait
In the sand, glowing red — even
His blood didn't wash the culprits
Clean. In Rome, before the burning,
The executioners nailed the tongue
Of Giordano Bruno, whose counsel they didn't
Want, who spoke to the people with his
Last word stolen. That proved
He was right: They had more grounds
Than he did to be afraid.

Reime

Allah warf in die Weltenmitte die
Sprache & sie zersplitterte zu
1000 Scherben
Die nicht zueinander
Passen wollten, zu Kerben
Im Namenlosen
Woraus generiert sich die
Genesung, wenn nicht aus Rosen?
Die Kälte wabert durch den Salon
Die Bise dringt durch Kittel
& T-Shirt, der vereiste Asphalt
Durch das dünne Leder
An den Sohlen
Kälte regiert empfindlich
Zigarettenrauch füllt die Lungenflügel
Wärmt schlecht, Philine fragte:
„Und wenn ich dich lieb habe
Was geht's dich an?"
Reime lieben sich, Verse überhaupt
Überhaupt sagt Poesie
Wahr, auch wenn sie von Johanni spricht
Vom Leuchten der weissen Rose
Im Tempel, von denen
Die da Weisheit haben
& Kraft & Kunst
Wo suchen wir? Im
Dunkel erglänzenden
Firmament.

Rhymes

Allah cast the word into the midst of the
World and it splintered into
1000 shards
That would not fit together, to nooks
In the nameless
Whence recovery generated,
If not from the rose?
The chill swirls through the salon
The northwind pierces through coat
& T-Shirt, the iced asphalt
Through the thin leather
Of the soles
Chill governs delicately
Cigarette smoke fills the lungspan,
Warms badly, Philine asks:
"And if I held you dear
What would it be to you?"
Rhymes make love, especially in verse
Poesy especially speaks prophecies
When she also speaks of the Solstice Fest too
Of the light of the white rose
In the temple of those who
Have wisdom
& power & art
Where do we seek? In
The dark glittering
Firmament.

Licht-Aug

für Marie Colvin
> *(*12. Jan. 1956 in Oyster Bay, NY*
> *† 22. Feb. 2012 in Homs, Syrien)*

Das Aus für die Colvin
War ein Aus für das Licht
Das ihr Eines Auge
Für alle anderen
Entzündet

Es heisst
Sie habe
Leicht
Geliebt

Sie fand den Schlüssel
Zur gezeitigten Geborgenheit
Leicht
Ob all der Ungeborgenheit

Das stelle ich mir schön vor:

Auf einem Balkon in der Nähe
Des Tahrir-Platzes mit Marie
Colvin einen Wodka Martini
Heben, on the rocks
Nach einem anstrengenden Job
& dann zusammen duschen
& noch nass unter die Leintücher schlüpfen

Eye of Light

for Marie Colvin

*(*Jan. 12, 1956 in Oyster Bay, NY*
†Feb. 22, 2012 in Homs, Syria)

The out for Colvin
Was an out for the light
That her single eye
Ignited
For all others

It's said
She'd
Loved
Lightly

She found the key
To the resulting concealment
Lightly
Though all were unconcealed

I imagine this well:

On a balcony close to
Tahrir Square with Marie
Colvin lifting a vodka martini,
On the rocks
After an exhausting job
& showering together
& slipping wet under the sheets

Das Licht, das sie
Für alle anderen
Entzündet

Assads
Thron
Zittert
Unter
Ihrem
Licht-Aug

The light that she'd
Ignited
For all others

Assad's
Throne
Trembles
Under
Her
Eye of light

Die Schlange

Die Schlange machte Eurydike den Garaus
Als sie barfuss zur Kasse gebeten wurde
Auch da war es keine Frage des Alters
Eurydike musste hinab, zweimal

& Eva war offen für die Einflüsterungen der
    Klugen
Verlangte nach dem Apfel der Erkenntnis, viel
Intelligenter als Adam, der erst überzeugt
Werden musste, sie – geschaffen aus dem
    edlen
Rippenstoff, nicht aus Lehm, Dreck & Torf
Eva – die wahre Krone der Schöpfung

Den Rumpf auf der Erde, chthonisch durch &
    durch
Den Kopf leicht erhoben, züngelnd
In Höhlen & im Schatten mächtiger Steine, am
    Wegrand
Wohnend, wartet sie auf den Feind, die Beute

The Serpent

The serpent finished off Eurydike
When she was called barefoot for payment
And there was no question of age
Eurydike had to go down twice

& Eve was open to the blandishments of the
      clever
Yearned for the apple of consciousness, far
More intelligent than Adam, who at first needed
To be convinced, she—created from the stuff of
      his noble
Rib, not from clay, dung & dirt
Eve—the real crown of creation

The body on the ground, chthonic through &
      through
Lifted its head lightly, tonguing
In caverns and the shadow of mighty stone,
      dwelling
At the wayside, awaiting the enemy, the prey

CREDITS / CRÉDITOS / KREDÍTS

An Afternoon with Ed Sanders / Jackie Brown / On an Old Photograph / Old Love Song // Altes Liebeslied / Auf eine alte Fotografie / Ein Nachmittag bei Ed Sanders / Jackie Brown. In: Gobshite Quarterly / Issue 27-28 / Double Trouble (Ed.: R.V. Branham). Portland, Oregon, Summer-Fall 2017

An Afternoon with Ed Sanders / The Stone / Ein Nachmittag bei Ed Sanders / Der Stein (translation, Douglas Spangle). Cold Turkey Press. Sonnac 2019

Beer Poem (translated, Douglas Spangle). In: Christoph Keller (Ed.): Hip Hops – Poems About Beer. Everyman's Library Pocket Poets, Alfred A. Knopf. New York / Toronto 2018

Altes Liebeslied. In: Morgana Beat Anthologie Nr. 1. Leipzig, März 2007

Auf eine alte Fotografie / Jackie Brown / 17 Minuten in der Sauna. Florian Vetsch: 43 neue Gedichte. Songdog Verlag. Wien 2009

Blaubeerenparadies ungestillt / Intermezzo. Claire Plassard & Florian Vetsch: Ein dünner Faden hält alles zusammen / Ein Gedichtzyklus. Mit Zeichnungen von Harald Häuser und einem Auftakt von Katharina Franck. Moloko Print. Pretzien 2019

Der Stein / Die Schlange / Licht-Aug. Claire Plassard & Florian Vetsch: Steinwürfe ins Lichtaug / Ein Gedichtzyklus. Mit Zeichnungen von Harald Häuser und einem Nachwort von Felix Philipp Ingold. Moloko Print. Pretzien 2014

Die Häutung des Marsyas. Hadayatullah Hübsch & Florian Vetsch: Round & Round & Round / Ein Gedichtzyklus. Songdog Verlag. Wien 2011

Die toten Dichter. Florian Vetsch: Untote auf der Stör. Gonzo Verlag. Verstreute Gedichte VIII. Mainz 2016

Ein Gedicht. Florian Vetsch: Die Feuertränke / Ausgewählte Gedichte 1984–1997. Rohstoff Verlag. Herdecke 2002

Ein Nachmittag bei Ed Sanders. Florian Vetsch: Im Ledig House / Ein Frühling in New York. Books Ex Oriente (Edition Occidente). München 2012

Reime. Hadayatullah Hübsch & Florian Vetsch: Eis bricht leis / 6 Gedichte. Gonzo Verlag. Verstreute Gedichte II. Mainz 2013

Con respecto a una vieja fotografía, Traducción, T. Warburton y Bajo y rvb; Jackie Brown, Traducción, T. Warburton y Bajo y rvb; Vieja canción de amor, Traducción, T. Warburton y Bajo y rvb y Lyda Alvarez; Una tarde con Ed Sanders, Traducción, T. Warburton y Bajo y rvb; Traducción, T. Warburton y Bajo y rvb; In: Gobshite Quarterly / Issue 27-28 / Double Trouble (Ed.: R.V. Branham). Portland, Oregon, Summer-Fall 2017

O staroj fotografiji, prijevod, Ana Katana; Jackie Brown, Prijevod, Jelena Pataki; Stara ljubavna pjesma, prijevod, Ana Katana; In: Gobshite Quarterly / Issue 27-28 / Double Trouble (Ed.: R.V. Branham). Portland, Oregon, Summer-Fall 2017

Titelverzeichnis

Verzeichnis der Gedichtanfänge

Índice de títulos

○ ○ ○ ○ ○ ○ ○ ○ ○ ○ ○ ○ ○ ○ ○ ○ ○ ○

Índice de primeras líneas

*) *Traducción, T. Warburton y Bajo y rvb;*
**) *Traducción, T. Warburton y Bajo y rvb y Lyda Alvarez*

○ ○ ○ ○ ○ ○ ○ ○ ○ ○ ○ ○ ○ ○ ○ ○ ○ ○

‡) *Prijevod, Ana Katana;*
‡‡) *Prijevod, Jelena Pataki*

Display type set in Didot, **HITCHCOCK**, **JEAN LUC**, Mona Lisa, Palatino HERCULENIUM, & Sabon, except when not.

Georgia is used for punctuation in conjunction with Sabon or Palatino texts, except when not; headings set in Palatino, except when set in Didot, or Mona Lisa, or another font; Epigraphs set in Didot or Sabon, except when not.

BIOS

Swiss writer Florian Vetsch (b. 1960) has published poetry, diaries, essays and anthologies. His most recent works include a poetic collaboration with the artist Peter Z. Herzog, *Sapphische Flaschenpost* (Vexer, Berlin/St.Gallen 2016); the cult reader *Tanger Telegramm* (Bilger, Zurich 2004/2017), an anthology of literature on the Moroccan city of Tangier which he co-edited with Boris Kerenski; *A Night in Zurich* (Gonzo, Mainz 2018), a bilingual and illustrated collaboration with Ira Cohen and Jürgen Ploog; *Ein dünner Faden hält alles zusammen* (Moloko Print, Schönebeck 2019), the second cycle of poems he wrote in exchange with the poet Claire Plassard, with drawings by Harald Häuser and an introduction by the singer-songwriter Katharina Franck; his poetry volume *Quintessenz* (San Marco Handpresse, Neustadt 2020), with color etchings by Peter Marggraf, *&* a bilingual edition of Paul Bowles's theater piece *The Garden* (Bilger, Zurich 2022), designed by Dario Benassa.

Florian Vetsch has translated works by Jack Black, Lawrence Ferlinghetti, Allen Ginsberg, Jan Heller Levi, Jan Herman, Louise Landes Levi, Mohammed Mrabet, Mark Strand, Janine Pommy Vega, Anne Waldman, and others. He teaches Philosophy and German Literature at the Kantonsschule am Burggraben in St.Gallen where he lives with his family.

Douglas Spangle, born in Roanoke, Virginia, *&* raised in a Park Service family, spent his childhood in various western states before his family moved overseas. He finished high school in Ankara, Turkey, *&* attended University of Maryland's Munich Campus (1968-1971). He spent the next four years as a stagehand at the Münchener Kammerspiele Schauspielhaus.

He has been involved in all aspects of Portland's poetry scene, curating city-wide poetry *&* cultural events such as ArtQuake, co-editing *Rain City Review*, hosting open mic series at Satyricon *&* other venues, hosting the widely popular, decade-long open mic at Café Lena. His many chapbooks include a translation of Friedrich Hölderlin's poetry, *Blood and Wine* (Fly Leaf eds., 2008). Author of *A White Concrete Day: Poems, 1978-2013*, and recipient of Oregon Literary Arts' Stewart H. Holbrook Literary Legacy Award, he is currently translating Swiss authors Christoph Keller, Florian Vetsch, *&* Clemens Umbricht for *Gobshite Quarterly, Reprobate/GobQ Books, &* various Swiss anthologies.

Lyda Alvarez, who's been entertaining people in PDX w/ her wry *&* mordant readings, began writing erotica to amuse an incarcerated friend, *&* subsequently had work in *Gobbshite Quarterly*.   Lyda has also done Spanish translation copy-editing, as well as working with T. Warburton y Bajo *&* rvb on Spanish translations, one of which is included in this volume. Originally fr. Monterrey, Mex., Lyda works as a hairstylist.

RV Branham has two fiction collections, *Chango Chingamadre & Other Moral Fictions*, & *A New Order of the Phylum* (Seventh Station Books); he's also the author/compiler of *Curse+Berate in 69+ Languages* (Soft Skull Press, 2nd printing). His fiction has been been translated in such journals as

Poetinis Druskininkų Ruduo (Lithuania) and *Tema* (Croatia), as well as Japanese & German editions of Gardner Dozois anthologies. His fiction, essays & pomes have been in publications & anthologies, such as *Red Lemonade's Hybrid Beasts* e-book, *Ellery Queen's Mystery Magazine, Isaac Asimov's SF Mag., 2 gyrls quarterly, In Other Words Mérida, Unlikely Stories* and *The Writing Disorder*. Translator as well as writer, for twenty years R.V.'s been publishing editor of the completely multilingual en-face *Gobshite Quarterly* (in double issue flip-book format) & publishing editor of *GobQ/Reprobate Books*.

Ana Katana, teacher & translator of English & Italian, lives in Zagreb, Croatia. with their spouse & eight-year old son. In addition to doing extensive Croatian translations for *Gobshite Quarterly*, Ana has also translated approx. 30 novels, mostly for young adults, by authors like Victoria Aveyard, Jordan Ifueko, Rebecca Roanhorse. Ana travels, hikes & jogs with their family, & collects vinlyl everything from The Highwaymen, Kris Kristofferson and Johnny Cash to their absolute favourite, Nick Cave, followed by Florence Welch, and Francesco de Gregori; also loving David Bowie, Fleetwood Mac, Depeche Mode, The National, &Meatloaf. Others incl. ex-Yugoslavian acts such as Haustor & Partibrejkers.

Jelena Pataki Šumiga is a TA at the Faculty of Humanities & Social Sciences, University of Osijek, Croatia, where she teaches courses on Old English literature & contemporary British dystopia. She wrote her PhD thesis on the abuse of the body in contemporary Anglophone dystopias, & her wider field of study is Anglophone literature & (popular) culture, with an emphasis on YA, dystopia & fantasy. She is a member of the YA Studies Assn., Utopian Studies Society Europe, Croatian Assn. for the Study of English, & Croatian Assn. for American Studies, a member of the Executive Committee of the Centre for Popular Culture at the University of Osijek & co-editor of its scholarly blog *Fractals: The Shapes of Popular Culture*. As a member of the Croatian Literary Translators Assn., she has translated more than fifty novels from English to Croatian for several Croatian publishers.

T. Warburton y Bajo's work history includes translation, newspaper & magazine design, photo editing, & art criticism. They've been an assoc. editor & designer w/ GobQ since 2001. Their experience also includes working as a translator & interpreter., & photo-researcher. They devide their time betwixt Baja California, Brit. Columbia. They collaborated on all of the Spanish translations of the pomes in this collection.

Studying under Florian Vetsch, Temea Wissmann (b. 2001) discovered their interest in philosophy. Upon graduation, they plan to work in theatre & the performing arts. Their portrait of Florian is on page 3.